# Enneagram

## *Patterns & Poetics*

A guide to understanding personality

# Copyright

www.enneagrampoetics.com

# Dedicated to

my clients—to our relationships,
and to the sacred space
from which the self is renewed.

# Enneagram Patterns & Poetics

# Overview

The material and design language in *Enneagram Patterns & Poetics* is an outgrowth of what is found in our mobile application EnneaApp, originally released in 2013. If you are new to The Enneagram, it may be helpful to first familiarize yourself with The Enneagram via the introductory descriptions found in EnneaApp. The intention with this book is to provide a more overarching understanding of The Enneagram as a complete and holistic System of Personality.

The language in EnneaApp has been left intact to honor the tradition and lineage from which it emerged. The reader familiar with both may notice differences and departures. That in mind, both sources can stand alone, or work together in your study of The Enneagram. Our hope is that you find both useful in different ways and that they serve as complimentary resources, each pointing in their own way to the wisdom of self-discovery.

This book is broken up into four sections:

Part I - The Patterns
*The Energy and Intelligences that shape personality*

Part II - The Types
*The archetypal patterns of The Enneagram*

Part III - The Context
*The impact of life and circumstance on personality*

Part IV - The Details
*Key details of the nine Primary Types*

The reason for this order is to indicate that The Enneagram is best understood as a system. The complex and dynamic personalities presented by The Enneagram are all built of the same basic elements. Understanding the component parts allows for a fuller understanding of the whole. As such, the first three sections move from narrow to broad in their focus. The last section is designed for quick and easy reference.

The suggestion is to first read through the book in order. Thereafter, flip around however you like. Connect in your own way with the images and the different aspects of the patterns. The elements of typology and personality contained here are only reflections of what is lived and felt in the individual and in the collective.

# Preface

The writing is broken up into bits
these are meant to help you
experience and construct
your own understanding of
The Enneagram
System of Personality,
and the patterns therein.
The style is intended to be
contemplative writing with imagery,
poetry with a dash of
short-hand psychoeducation.
Though the words
have been carefully chosen,
they are but signposts—
it is by and of the reader
that they are brought to life.

The intention is to go inward
as a moment calls,
to find your own way
to attend to the interplay
between compassion and understanding,
to know more of what you are working with,
in whatever way that may be.
The Enneagram is one of many
systems of understanding—
ways of making meaning,
it can be a part of your path,
an approach you weave in and out of,
or not your language at all.

Only you know who you are
and what resonates in your being.
My perspective is that of
a therapist, educator and poet
though foremost I know
I am a student.
It was always the teacher
who reminded of *both*
the known and unknown,
of life and learning
folding into one another.
It was from that edge
they passed down
the many years of study,
the container they held
as it held space
for the moment.

Thank you to the guides,
to the fellow-travelers,
to those fierce with kindness
who knew and lived the archetypes in a way
that reflected the essence of what it means
to always be growing into more of what we
were always becoming,
and of what it is to come home
to that unbounded space of spirit.

# PART I—*The Patterns*

The Energy and Intelligences that shape personality

This section addresses the drives and forces behind personality formation. The Enneagram is a dance of psychology and spirituality. While the poetry is aimed at the ethereal, the descriptions of Enneagram aspects are written as concretely as possible. Regardless, the terms selected are less important than the concepts they point to.

# Provenance

There you are
all the eras and epochs
expansions of light and darkness
of form and the surrounding context.
Everything, everywhere
and nowhere at all,
-unfolding all together-
be still a moment
and know thyself.

# Energy

Life begins with a surge of energy,
-of what it means to come *into* being-
to grow means to participate in the flow of energy,
and so to exist is to contain energetic capacities—
those within, and those all around.
We are always encountering, relating
and being renewed again.

# Instincts

Our instincts signify the way we
as human beings
apply energy towards
the most fundamental of imperatives: *survive.*
The first line of code paves way to the others:
movement, growth, change, connection. Everything.
To survive is to begin to thrive.
And so our instincts are always
on that razor's edge
where we experience
the immediacy of our aliveness.

For human beings, *surviving & thriving* involves three main instincts. These instincts represent exchanges of energy that occur between:

Self & Form - First and foremost, the corporeal aspects of the self must be protected and nourished. We all need food, water, shelter, sleep, etc. We all must seek and manage resources that contribute to our personal homeostasis. The aim of this energy is *preservation*. Down to the level of our cells, we are programmed to work on the repair and maintenance of our inner systems so as to be able to move, grow and adapt as need be.

Self & Other - The deepest and strongest bonds we make are in one-to-one relationships. The aim of this energy is *generation*. We grow from pairs—even our genes and our chromosomes come in pairs. In the same way that a straight line is the shortest distance between two points, this energy represents a focused form of energy. Note—this instinct points not at the self or other, but rather at that which is created between them.

Self & Group - We come into the world already knowing the voices of our families. We see the world through the collective paradigms that we participate in. Human beings are social creatures. The aim of this energy is *interconnection*. To evolve we must work together. We live amidst the emergent properties. This instinct speaks of the sum that is greater than the parts.

Though we may shift the way we relate to our Instincts, the energy that fuels them is always fundamental and foundational.

The Instincts each have a different wavelength, and therefore
a different felt sense:

Self & Form is the humdrum
pulling in upon itself,
it is the underlying attention
an insular and buzzing busyness
dispersed steadily along the plain.

Self & Other is the sizzling
the spark of intensity,
the electricity of first contact
the potential to be taken over, set ablaze—
it is the crescendo that gives way to resetting.

Self & Group is a tuning into,
a staying with the melodies and the harmonies,
the key that informs the composition,
it is the knowing of resonance and dissonance
reverberating out towards the circumference.

# Instinct Set

A complete Instinct Set contains all 3 energetic patterns.

Primary Instinct - The predominant energy in the body; the Instinct most heavily relied on.

Secondary Instinct - The energy that supplements and compliments the primary instinctual strategy.

Tertiary Instinct - The least distributed energetic pattern; the under-utilized instinctual capacity.

A Primary Instinct will have two main variations depending on which Instinct is secondary. There are endless distributions and manifestations of these energies.

Self & Form - This Instinct Set holds that attention to *preservation* necessarily precedes attention to *generation* and *interconnection.*

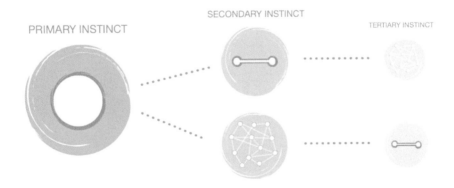

PRIMARY INSTINCT

SECONDARY INSTINCT

TERTIARY INSTINCT

Self & Other - This Instinct Set holds that *generation* represents the seeds for further *preservation* and *interconnection*.

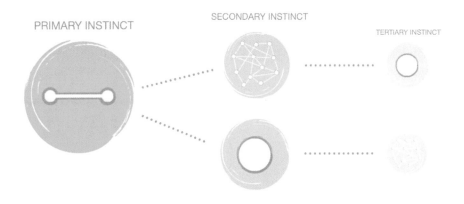

Self & Group - This Instinct Set holds that *interconnection* encompasses and transcends the needs for *preservation* and *generation*.

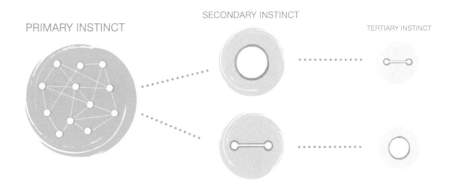

# Centers

Energy, in the physical world is encoded with information.
To understand information is to have intelligence.
Human beings have three basic intelligence centers.

Gut - *Somatic Intelligence* - The most immediate and fundamental experience of ourselves, accessed via sensate awareness. To be is to have the gut intelligence of the body. The gut is the intelligence closest to the Instincts.

Heart - *Emotional Intelligence* - The heart is where we know ourselves and connect most deeply. Emotions are the forces that animate personality, build relationships and give our lives meaning.

Head - *Mental Intelligence* - The ability to gather, sort, analyze and interpret. It is from the head that we can build upon or refine information and work with conceptual frameworks.

While the different intelligences occur as distinct, all three must work in tandem, each containing aspects of one another.

Like the Instincts, each of the Centers contains their own unique experiential quality:

In the gut, impulses fire
a preliminary, decisive movement
in a certain and singular direction.
They occur at the core
and move us out, into action.

In the heart, feelings grow
pulling in and towards
they expand, well up inside us,
and, sometimes, break us open.
They are the palette that colors our world.

In the head, thoughts proliferate
a flurry of cerebral activity
tangential, this way, suddenly that,
moving rapidly along neural pathways—
those familiar and those waiting to light up.

Though the intelligences themselves are neutral, we navigate our use of them in a threatening world. To be moved by these intelligences is to do the hard work of being human.

Given the quantity of information all around, we typically filter and process information very rapidly. We rely on the implicit knowledge of what our intelligences automatically prime us to seek and avoid.

Remembering and learning from pain is essential to survival. Each Center of Intelligence is responsible for managing a painful aspect of our inner and outer world.

Ultimately, our centers prompt us to respond to life and challenge us to stay true to ourselves.

The Gut manages *anger*. Anger reminds us of what we value most and what our limits are. Anger is a natural response to that which is unjust; it is the muscle that seeks *fairness*.

The Heart manages *shame*. Shame is connected to our basic need to know and demonstrate our *worthiness* as we relate to ourselves, others and our environment.

The Head manages *fear*. Our survival necessitates recognizing and responding to fear. The aim of addressing fear represents a search for *security*.

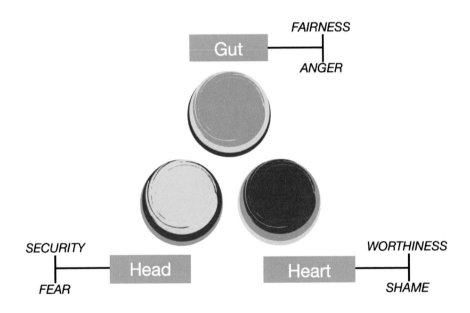

Centers are the underpinnings of strategy—
adaptive and dynamic intelligences,
organized towards needs
and away from pain.

# The Symbol

The three centers
create the inner triangle.

Each pattern contains three variations—
these are the three triads
that make up the nine patterns
found along the circumference.

The remaining six connections
each find their own necessary
counterparts and balancing forces
defining the inner hexagram.

# The Enneagram

The Enneagram is told
in the narrative tradition—
it is built from the stories
calling out to be heard.
To write is to know that ultimately
the writer surrenders
to the limits of language.
The map is not the terrain,
though it allows the traveler to find
their way in and out.
The Enneagram symbol is passed down
from one generation to another.
To study then, is to share in the work.

The Enneagram is a route into
discovery and understanding,
a looking through and into and upon
the personal and universal strategies,
the ways of being, of meeting needs,
avoiding pain, relating to life.
There is no destination
to pattern recognition
it is simply heard, seen, felt, lived.
The multitudes are to be experienced,
for the *self* is always there—
at the surface, down in the layers,
folded deep into the subtleties,
waiting to be known, once again.

# PART II—*The Types*

The archetypal patterns of The Enneagram

The identification of an Enneagram Type represents not only a Primary Type, but also a set of complimentary patterns working together in a particular way. This section begins by detailing the basic Enneagram personality structure, and then moves into a piece on each of the Nine Types.

The order of the latter half of this section is designed to point to a fundamental aspect of the Type's formation within the larger system. While the Centers are still grouped together, the Types themselves are arranged non-linearly. The intention behind this particular order is to further articulate how the Types are interconnected, one pattern necessitating another.

# Circles

In the circle we see wholeness,
a representation of how
every aspect of The Enneagram
is inextricably linked,
a type always feeding into another,
inhabiting whatever particular location
amidst the infinite points
that make up the circumference.
Our lived experience,
what it means to navigate our world,
always exists in unison with life
and the continuity of all things.
The lens, the perspective, the vantage point
represents a personal center of gravity,
a distinct point of view
that we come to know as ours alone.

# Primary Types

The Primary Types are variances
of the nine archetypal patterns,
the manifestations of intelligence,
that we already know in our being.
They are there in the stories,
in the art, in the iterations
of the great wit.
They are how we move things along,
how we come into our own,
who we strive to be,
what makes up the space between.
Oh how we are alike
of one creation,
and how we are different...
the shackles, the armor, the tools
channels, frequencies
what we learned to use
and to manage and to let go of
and of course to find once again.
To know an archetype
is to know the system,
to really know a single pattern
is to understand the whole.

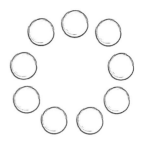

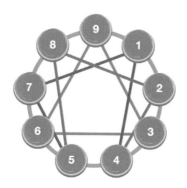

# Wings

Adjacent to the Primary Type are the Wings. The Wings color
our primary patterns, and therefore enrich our perspective.

Each of the nine points along the circle
has personality patterns on either side of it.
While we are impacted by all 9 archetypal patterns,
it is our neighboring patterns that are always at hand.
Our wings are with us as we move through life.
Typically we have an inclination or preference
towards one wing, or the other.
And while a wing will typically be dominant,
they reside on the same axel,
and so the lesser developed wing
represents a balancing force.

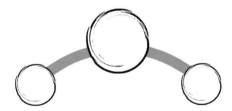

# Lines

Again the Primary Type has 2 connecting paths depicted in the Lines. The connected types are 'Points' that we find ourselves touching into, in one way or another.

In the lines we see
how the tapestry is woven—
the inner and outer dynamics,
the geometry
resting at the backdrop
of the archetypal patterns.

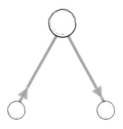

The pattern's 'Support Point' is the pattern we lean on when we need to supplement, bolster or offset the strategy of the Primary Type. *The arrow towards the Primary Type represents us bringing in or incorporating an alternative pattern.*

The pattern's 'Open Point' holds the potential for integration. Openness allows the Primary Type to be more present to the moment and to ourselves. *The arrow away from the Primary Type represents stepping into or making space for a new pattern.*

The lines reinforce
the interdependence of
the three centers
and the nine types.
This is the 'gram' of Enneagram,
a map that points to
the profound patterns behind
the dance of personality.

# Type Set

The Type Sets are primarily built around the gravitational center of the Primary Type.

*Each Set is made up of five patterns:* Primary Type (1) + Lines (2) + Wings (2)

Primary Type 'PT' - The personality pattern at the core of the individual. Our baseline rests somewhere along the outer circle, which represents our center of gravity. Our Primary Type is built around both what we *seek* and what we *avoid*.

Wings 'w'- The types we reside between on the outer circle. Our Primary Type tends to favor one of the adjacent wings.

*Each Primary Type is connected to two other types via the inner lines.*

Support Point 'SP' - The pattern the Primary Type leans on when needing reinforcement.

Open Point 'OP'- The pattern that allows for integration and equilibrium in the Primary Type.

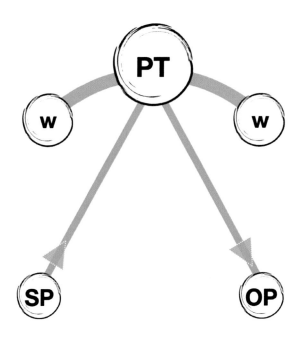

*For detailed Type Sets (including arrow 'Point' indicators) flip to PART IV - Details.*

# Personality Patterns

A Personality Type ends up as a description
created by attempting to capture
the thoughts, feelings and behaviors—
the motivations of the ego.
Detailing the patterns of personality
is the impossible task of
defining the essential qualities
of an ever-evolving strategy.
When we speak of type,
it is always as we see it
in the world and in ourselves.
And yet the patterns
are not the person
and the person is not just
a single particular pattern.
Within us and
within the collective
is the capacity to witness,
to see is to begin
to make space for
curiosity, growth, kindness—
when we understand the pattern,
we allow for that
which is beyond the habitual
ways of seeing.

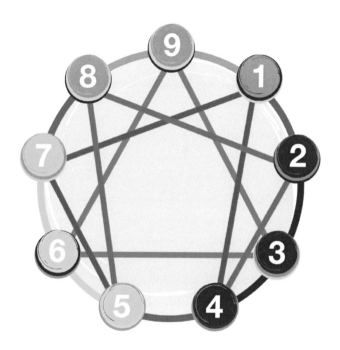

The remainder of this section consists of a look into the formation and perspective of each of the nine personality patterns.

# Type 9

Resting at top center
the initial archetype
the forgotten self in all of us
that has long since fallen asleep.
All nine patterns represent a
covering of one's true nature,
always awakening
and returning
to that present moment
from which we all leave
again and again.
9 relates to every pattern
as they are all
of the same forgotten self,
left adrift amidst the face
of an ever unknowable whole.
To understand the 9 pattern is to
experience the interdependence
of the three Centers of Intelligence,
how they both
build momentum *and*
wrestle inertia.
The (forgotten) power of the 9
is that it is the most immediately positioned—
it is closest to the raw energy
that fuels the instincts.
9 contains the broadest view
and the most experiential understanding
of all the patterns of the system,
a center of mass that incorporates
the surrounding circles and spirals.

The irony is that indolence
quickly becomes
an active and demanding process,
a ritual of favoring a known comfort
at the cost of a deeper satisfaction.
Entrenchment in tranquility
leads to an inevitable and necessary
sense of dis-ease,
a waking up, in a way
to an unnamed tension…
stirrings and rumblings
giving way to a restless remembrance
of the true authorship of our lives—
that the self alone must
take this road or that.

To move into
a greater sense of presence
initially involves a willingness
to stay steadily outside
and steadfastly aware
of the pull towards the habitual.
It is only in attendance to what is
that the self can be known,
the direction or preference named
the opinion decided upon
and purposefully understood.
In the radiance of awareness
rests the gracious embrace
of the beloved self.

# Type 8

8 represents an antithesis
to the falling asleep at 9.
It is the pattern that projects
an excess of life force—
to engage the charge
is to harness it,
to channel the charge
is to know aliveness
and the unbounded capacity
of one's life force.
To stand
is to have a stance
and in such a position
our truth is revealed.
Life is lived at the threshold,
the intensity of that razor's edge
where self-determination
is the known and felt
impact that we have
on the world.
Through ourselves, others and the world
we make our presence known.
It is here, in the reverberations of being
that leads the way towards
the immutable power of instinct.
To survive then is to protect
our space, our selves,
those who are closest
and those who are
tried and true.

Control is the illusion
that seems determined
to make demands of
that which is elusive and ephemeral
beyond one's boundaries
past the limits, pacing
protecting the perimeter
amidst the terrain
where a natural order of instincts
invariably takes a toll.
Sheer force all but
carves out it's own weakness,
and so away to
the position of retreat
to re-grouping and
letting the muscles breathe
collecting thoughts
and standing strong
once again.

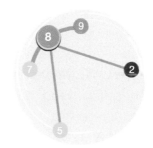

Innocence is the gentle,
timeless reminder that
it's okay to breath deep
to let go of the shackles
of my way and my terms
and to instead be made fuller
by the vulnerability,
to step into the truth
and into the immediate, expansive
nature of surrender,
feeling into
the life force
that fuels the will.

# Type 1

1 represents the valiant attempt
to bring focus to the disorder of 9
and manage the
impulsivity at 8.
Our unmeasured self
can bring chaos and destruction
and so the aim of the 1
is to balance the scale
with structure and order,
the maintenance of which requires
discipline and steadfastness,
a strength of holding all the tension
that the gut brings.
1's contained anger lives between the
expressed anger of the 8
and the repressed anger of the 9.
Type 1 represents the illusion of control—
of how life should go, and how best
to manage and maintain
the struggle with entropy
that is all around.
And still though
we all must choose
what is right for us
and seek the path of integrity
with ourselves and what we stand for.

The disorientation of disorder
lends to the way things should be,
or could be, or would be
if we would all just
be willing to hold it all together.

There is a way
to do this and that
or to do that which has
ultimately been decided to be
in the judgment of it all—good.
But somehow,
not good enough.
And so conviction tightens,
inner and outer workings
persistent in that all-consuming
task at hand
where we diligently attend
to what is good and tried
and true and worthy
right and righteous
black and white
written and recorded
on the mantel of life.

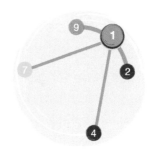

The softening is built in—
it is to see that to let go
is only to realize that we
never held on to begin with.
However perfectly the note was struck
and intricately the song created
there was always a
glimmer of radiance
a beauty beyond
a joy that breaks open
and out, and into life.
Plain and simple
and still somehow unexplainable,
a sense of serenity
resting deep inside.

# Type 6

The self-forgetting nature
of personality formation
leaves us feeling lost
wandering amidst danger and threat
in a world and with a body
that seems fundamentally fragile
like spun glass—
or worse, outright threatening
tossing and turning in unpredictability
so much uncertainty
in which there is always
the choices to waffle between
a wave function to collapse
as we walk trepidly into the unknown
avoiding that which reminds us of
existential realities past and present
real and imagined, and so either way
saddle up and gather
your stitched-together supplies
your pledge of loyalty
as we head on to that
cautious search for safety.
There, to all, is some basic fear
which the personality is defending against
the immediacy of fear
that all patterns know…
that simple awareness—
that life and death
are inextricably linked,
one always giving way to the other.
6 then is the remembrance that
paradox and polarity are ever present,

that all things of this world change
and that we must be with questions
that have answers unknown.

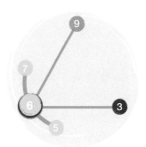

Hypervigilant yet distracted
synapses and cortisol
anxiety builds images of
falling and crumbling
of how the untended dam
always breaks.
Busy is the body that seeks
security through production,
safety in consistency,
and drives, all the while
yearning for worth, played out
in capacity, commitment
and the scattered dimensions of
being and doing.

And so, breathing into the body
and breathing out,
stillness as the top spins
and then of its own accord, rolls over,
letting things be for a moment
and a moment more.
Breathing in again to see
that it's okay,
and it's going to be okay,
in the gleam of trust
a unity underlying the polarity,
convergence *with* harmony
and that unchanging sense
of stillness and peace—
waiting all along
under the restless waves.

# Type 7

The overwhelming darkness
in the cosmos,
the unknowns resting at 6
leaves the seeker
bound, in a way, to focus on the light
on the emergence of joy and presence
where it is especially
good to be alive
where light and life delight
and the fruit is so ripe
giving way, this way and that—
those fits of laughter
so funny it almost hurts
so happy to be here
right now, right now—
or if not, soon enough
-about to be-
that planned *now*...
In the face of the existential
and the ever-demanding task
of moving through the world
why not lean-in-to
the sparks, the fire
the embers,
and those eagerly anticipated
moments of magic.

Wanting gives way to
wanting more,
doing more and overdoing
another high
rivaling the zest of the last

seeking and craving and chasing
an eager yet
frustrated state of being
high strung
a half-beat ahead
avoiding a certain
sinking feeling
containment makes space
for a plan in mind,
a way to move forward
a map to be made
of the journey to be had.

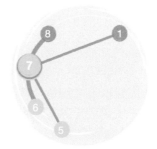

The discovery waiting in plain sight
is that freedom is only possible
with balance and discernment.
To work is to commit to the
steady effort of building habits
finding consistency,
discovering the wonder
of truly attending
to a course of action.
To be fully present
to the spectrum of life
is the ground from which
all vision and joy emerges.

# Type 5

The pattern of 5 represents
an attendance to the key
mechanisms of intelligence.
Here we find the path of
deciphering and utilizing
the information embedded in the energy
that is ever-present.
To consistently focus on
what is known or knowable
is to balance
the precarious and precocious
patterns at 6 and 7.
To look closely enough
at anything
is to discover a world
waiting to be explored and investigated,
documented and retained for reference.
And so undisturbed
one must remain
to manage the steadfastness
of gathering information,
sifting out the hidden biases—
the misconceptions and misunderstandings,
the operator errors that come with being human.

In a world that is ultimately
unknowable and unpredictable,
resources must be managed,
and expenditures calculated—
for objectivity exacts
a seemingly high price.
Distance to safely

and carefully observe is
a self-protective measure.
Space is then for gazing upon,
sitting outside the panorama
wanting to know the world
but reluctant to share.
If not far out and away then
zoomed all the way in to those
most granular of details.

Engagement cuts through
snapping the watcher
up and out of detachment
and into a more immediate perception,
a participation in the experience,
a dance with the great beautiful mystery.
It is the embodied knowing of what it is
to give and share more freely
to respond and to know how
to take up space,
to be empowered,
settling into the
open and generous reminder
that knowing *is* remembering
and that we are all a part
of the full-circle
of universal knowledge.

# Type 3

The core pattern of any personality
is a fabrication, an invented self
where the fear of being lost
gets converted into an identity
that attaches to the possibility
of gaining that which one has forgotten is inherent,
and of impressing that worthiness
upon the beholder.
It is the chasing of illusive ends
that forages for the illusioned self,
stuck believing that to go on
is the same as to go on pretending.
Progression then becomes measured
by the impact of our efforts—
success alone is not enough,
the sustainability of continued investment
is justified by increased output.
As we generate we strive
towards more efficient, and therefore,
more generative ends.
This pattern speaks to finesse,
to that elegant way
of moving things towards
the finish line, goal, target
to whatever is seen now
and sought on the horizon.

Pursuit of an external metric
sooner or later leaves the seeker
in an energized yet tiresome condition.
All-in, at the edge of the wick of burnout
racing past the clock, busy in

conceiving, perceiving and deceiving
that seen, projected image—
a winner to be valorized
a path to be paved then bejeweled
breaking forth,
in the name of aspirations.
A focus on the ends tends to lend to
spinning and circuitous routes,
a dance of decorum,
selling and buying ego boosts
of shimmering magnanimity.

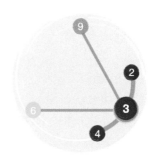

Growth finds its way in
cracks and crevices,
past the perceived missteps
is the emergent self
waiting to be witnessed anew
patiently abiding
just under the surface
and all the way down
to the depths of being
reflected only in the light of true seeing.
At the core of emotion and honesty—
a healthy sense of self-assurance,
and the effortless nature of
letting go, letting in and letting up
choosing instead to be
carried along by the task
by that greater than the self,
aligned with the laws
of effort and will.
To know thyself
is to know the stillness from which
being and becoming are born.

# Type 4

4 represents
that tender process
of what it means to have a heart
broken open to life, to beauty,
and to the intuition
that is waiting both inside
and out there...
scribed in the tales
of anima and animus,
the one who is
following those same stars,
stepping closer and going inward.
To embark in such a way
is to begin to embrace an
individual essence,
to pay close and personal attention
so that the private, luminous mysteries
hidden therein might be revealed and revered.
Inauthenticity strikes of dissonance,
an avoidance of vulnerability
underneath which is the call for inner-work
of inhabiting the indelible authentic self.
Such labor is done in the forest—
the ever shifting terrain
teeming with biodiversity
and waves of light that go unseen to most.
The path of 4 is to know innately
of the wind delicately brushing past
and rustling those still and shimmering waters.
The landscape changes as night approaches
where those same woods now glow in the twilight
and the lake runs as deep as the night sky it reflects.

Lost inwardly,
the flawed-self preoccupied
with the stage, the stories
the myriad of individuals
at the heart beat of it all
alive in yearning and longing
shaking and awakening
finding meaning and significance
fully immersed in the
whirling ways of the heart,
sometimes a melancholy
so layered and textured
one can't help but see
the special beauty waiting
to be heard, witnessed, known
in the depths of our being.

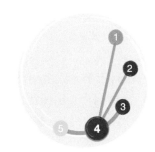

To discover equanimity
is to find presence in
the realistic assessment
that is beyond reaching and clutching.
It lives in identifying, defining and delineating
those transpersonal boundaries—what is of,
and what is outside of
the waves of the heart.
In the vastness of it all
beauty and abounding creativity
-fluid, flowing, and infinite-
all surrender to the
emergent layers of the fractal.

# Type 2

2 is the path of generosity
and open-heartedness.
The focus on the self
found at 3 and 4
is balanced by a focus
on the other.
To give freely, or mostly so,
what others might want or need
is to invite abundance.
To see the worthiness in another
is to peer into the reflected self.
Oh what it is to know how
innocently and purely
we all looked out for a mirror.
And so the dance of 2
is to tend and attend to
the space of primacy, connection
and to the beautiful interdependence
behind the blossoming
of life and love.

To know on behalf of another
speaks of carrying weight
and hoping to pave
the path for our kin.
So too, must you
yield a moment
and acknowledge
that which rests under
the tacit over-extension
and self-sacrifice,
a certain importance found

in steering and orchestrating
and leaning into
the heart's given labor of love,
raveled up and into
the exalted, adapted self,
feeling ahead of and around
managing yet beholden to
the attachment made
or bond duly formed.

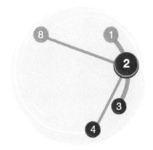

It is from equality
neither inflated nor deflated
that grace is known
inherent and innate
resting in the middle and
all along that forgotten boundary,
the poignant interface found
only by looking upon and honoring
the delineation and differentiation
of self and other.
It is the willingness to know the
true nature of hope and help,
a bedrock of worthiness
from which the self must emerge
and reclaim the freedom and power
waiting at the precipice of
the love that is always shared.

# PART III — *The Context*

The impact of life and circumstance on personality

While motivation and behavior are significant, a personality system must always be considered in light of a broader perspective. The Enneagram is only one small aspect of the layered and complex story of what it is to be alive in a particular space and time.

A study of the depths and subtleties of any person's experience will reveal that 'theory', ultimately, always falls short. The utility of The Enneagram is most accessible when held with the quality of openness, curiosity and a reverence for the unknown.

# Awareness

Awareness—in and of itself—breeds change.
As we move into awareness
we move closer to our true nature,
to the center of the circle, and outside it
into the capacity to observe.
Awareness is to create space
between stimulus and response.
The present is where we,
who we really are, is available.
Awareness is the quality
of contacting one's essence,
it is to remember that which
is impossible to forget,
because it is all there ever was.
The past is alive in the present
and what is to be unfolds of now.
The patterns and potentialities
of each personality are always here and now
waiting to be seen, named, understood,
transformed through awareness.
The things that make up our environment
are familiar just as the people we know;
it is only in looking closely that we can
see that which is calling out to be discovered.

Awareness is to be available to life.
It is in the present moment
where we experience our challenges,
our points of pain and suffering
our growth and evolution
what we cherish and savor,
our happiness, our deepest joys and gratitudes.

Our hearts beat in the here and now—
and so breathing in, breathing out
finding stillness and staying with…
This is the gift of bearing witness.

# Habituation

Our instincts and centers are honed with habits.
We use our energy and intelligences
to seek out our wants and needs
and to avoid pain, difficulty, harm.
Seeking and avoidance are tied together,
to speak of one is to invoke the other.
The increasing complexity of life
depends on the automaticity of many things,
an array of what must be
known, felt and actioned implicitly.
Our efforts, based on our motivations,
are simple—towards or away.
When we are successful in seeking and avoidance,
our habits are strengthened.
When we are unsuccessful
our habits are still strengthened.
The groove is built from the intention.
The intermittent reinforcement
brings its own unconscious
and preconscious momentum—
whatever we do we strengthen.

Changing a habit therefore requires
a willingness to be uncomfortable.
Change, as it is experienced in the present moment, is
physically, emotionally and neurologically more challenging
than traveling the familiar grooves of our personalities.
To create change we must stretch out space and time
and watch the seeking and avoidance arise
without necessarily (or immediately) indulging it.

It takes a certain stillness to recognize new ways of being,
it takes the practice of showing up again, and again
until the consistency enlightens us to the ease of change—
that what seemed like more work is actually less.
Initially challenging steps along a better path
become far easier in time.

# Conditioning

Just as our muscles, balance and circulation
are shaped by the planet's atmosphere,
so are our personalities
shaped within societal systems.
To understand these systems
we must look at the conditions,
the shared patterns within it—
the personal, familial, cultural, global,
so many collective
and exponential intersections
in a layered and dynamic process
it's hard to know what brushes are
coloring which details.
And still though, we certainly know of many
of the facets of our space and time.

We always see through our own biases.
Our habits and patterns, while being
essential to the nine archetypes
become particular and distinct,
nuanced to the self we were born into.
Our physical and social environments are
as alive as we are, and yet
the forces that surround us,
those that shape us,
they are not our core.
To understand our conditioning
is to know the responses pushing upwards,
the invitations that come with disinclinations
a certain fortitude amidst resistance
that we have been tasked to shoulder
as we set upon the contexts of our lives.

# Origins

The where, what and how of our beginnings—
of wanting and needing, belonging and mattering
reaching up, calling out for home
yearning for family,
the roots from which the vine unfurls.
It is the nature of origins to shape—
to both teach and scathe,
a piercing in, open and out
into the startling possibilities.
In the best of nurturance
are still the elements
and the harsh edges,
sinking moments with building tension
falling short and missing the mark
too much and not enough
a wound waiting to be witnessed
and a faculty embedded therein.

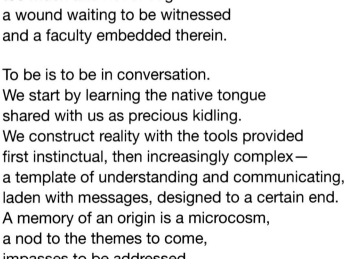

To be is to be in conversation.
We start by learning the native tongue
shared with us as precious kidling.
We construct reality with the tools provided
first instinctual, then increasingly complex—
a template of understanding and communicating,
laden with messages, designed to a certain end.
A memory of an origin is a microcosm,
a nod to the themes to come,
impasses to be addressed…
To look closely is to see that
under the weight of it all, past the faded scars
the innocence stills shines ever brightly.

# Narratives

The meaning we make
is informed by interpretations
lain over patterns.
Narratives of personality
speak to the categories and paradigms
that are built by following the personality's response
to shifting circumstances and dynamic situations.
Narratives of typology are the stories
that illuminate the stage on which we are playing.
They are the arcs embedded in the specifics,
the subtleties, the littlest details of our lives.
They are hidden in the self-perpetuating loops
that we both seek to keep exactly as they are,
and to change radically.

Narratives are seamed by
the internal and external
conversations of our lives.
They speak to the helical spirals of self-becoming.
Each pattern points to many courses of action
living in potentiality,
the story that we must engage in,
a true dilemma
a choice to be made
a superposition of possibility
that we look upon, live through,
and tell to the next generation.

# Processing

Though the entry point
may be most pronounced
in the head, heart or gut,
the work will always involve
the motions occurring in all three.
The particular process at hand
illuminates an individualized way
of weaving it all together.
To process is to organize,
move underneath, and see beyond.
It is the ability to both know and not know,
to breath in and out and through it.
To process is to allow for the movement
waiting to be witnessed.
Life is in motion.

Processing always occurs in the present
and yet involves the through-thread
of the self in time, as we experience it.
To process is to participate
in the work of finding alignment,
and so we process in tandem
with parts of ourselves,
with others, in groups, with life.
Processing requires
attending to and integrating
the intelligences of the centers.
To process means to be
willing to do the effortful work
of knowing, feeling and embodying
as well as the effortless work
of resting and abiding.

# Holding Space

Potential exists most strikingly
in the space of non-attachment
letting go of outcomes,
seeing what arises.
Holding is the embrace—
the corrective experience that is made possible
by allowing truth to find its own way forward.
We must explore without disturbing
we must be still and poised
ready for the unknown
so as to move through and towards
that which life is asking us to name,
to uncover that which is
just beyond the threshold of
who we know ourselves to be.
It is here where we meet that which
simply needs to be told,
seen, known, held
woven into the light.

The conversation, the contact
the energy exchange
the instincts, the centers, the patterns
all of being, contained
in a much larger space.
It is the space between
which holds all things.
And so, in the infinite expanse
we must contact the core
and stand by who we are,
all alone and held together.

# Intentionality

Intentions are set
within the framework
of the existing philosophy
and accompanying values.
To set intentions is to consider
how one may know and listen for
the sound resonating at the core
from which all is but an echo.

Intentions flow from intelligence—
each triad, in its own respective way
contributing to the projected future
and advocating why, in the face of all
that is unknown and unknowable,
it is still worth standing true
and laying our humble requests upon life.

To set intentions is to consciously take on
the positions, approaches and techniques
resting within and awaiting expression.
Intentionality is the active and steady work
of drawing and holding the bow
leaning into the moment, sustaining focus,
only to let go and follow through once more
where the final propulsion of energy
surrenders upon itself,
left only to trace the stars
and reflect the constellations
from which the brilliant expressions
of our light and life emerge.

# Relationships

Relationship represents
that which exists
of and from connection.
It is in relationship of any kind—
with others, with places
with the details
that make up spaces,
with the passing of time
and with the dynamic self,
that we are most deeply known.
Our very awareness
is inherently relational.
It is in that sacred space
of uncompromising aliveness
that life is illuminated.

Relationships are the growing, changing,
ever-evolving landscape,
they are the vibrant space where we find
both the edges and the heart of who we are.
Each encounter its own
world of possibility waiting to be
decided and co-created.
For any relationship to grow
it must be given energy,
we each must again
turn and move towards
or perhaps with and alongside
or against and away—
growing together, apart
and together again,
and so it is sewn.

Our inner dynamics
involve the ongoing
conversations and negotiations
between the parts of our being.
The Enneagram, and our particular,
highly-personalized patterns
contribute to the formation and management
of the parts of the self.
There is almost always some
inner conversation occurring,
differing degrees of resonance,
informing our state and perspective.
Integration involves both the differentiation of the parts,
as well as the understanding of mutuality—
of interdependence.

To focus inward then is to tend to a relationship
to the inner conversation of the moment.
The self is always understood
not separate from but alongside
the '&' that separates I from Thou
in that sacred space of all there is.

# Personal

To be alive is to know the pull
towards one's own
growth and change,
toward the expansion
that precedes the exhale.
The self alone knows
of the seeds planted, the subtle gifts
imprinted and bestowed upon us.
To be alive is to move out along
the cyclical and layered
concentric circles
etched in the timber of life force.
It is the aim and the sights set
the values beholden to
the hopes and fears
that speak to what matters most,
what is ours alone
is nothing more nor less
than the task, the function
the enigmatic purpose
the calling at hand,
hidden in plain sight
patiently awaiting the readiness
of our own self-actualization.

# Universal

All that surrounds
belongs to the same kingdom
infinitely reflected back upon itself.
The beauty and radiance of which
takes us up to the edge of the known,
to the startling precipice—
the perimeter that both
defines human limitation
and points to the great mystery
waiting just beyond the threshold,
past the preferences and circumstances
outside the particulars and concerns
of this or that pattern
is a more fundamental knowing
for to come through the improbabilities
and seeming impossibilities
is to find all along that tender embrace
of the dreamer gently awoken.

# PART IV — *The Details*

Key details of the nine Primary Types

This section contains specific characteristics of The Enneagram patterns mentioned throughout. The material here is organized for ease of access. The short-hand style is not for rote memory, but rather to give just enough indication for the reader to find their own inner connection to the patterns.

Some new terminology and descriptors are introduced to support a general understanding of the foundational and archetypal aspects of the Types and their interactions. This section also includes two new groupings ('Position' and 'Approach') which are useful ways of understanding how the patterns are both similar and different.

# Primary Aim

The Organizing Principle represents the patterns and drives that the Primary Type is built around.

This aim or motivating force leaves the Primary Type in a state of seeking, and thereby inclined to a preferred path or way forward.

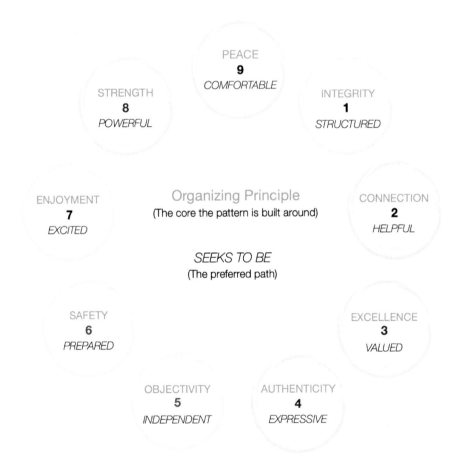

PEACE
**9**
*COMFORTABLE*

STRENGTH
**8**
*POWERFUL*

INTEGRITY
**1**
*STRUCTURED*

ENJOYMENT
**7**
*EXCITED*

Organizing Principle
(The core the pattern is built around)

CONNECTION
**2**
*HELPFUL*

*SEEKS TO BE*
(The preferred path)

SAFETY
**6**
*PREPARED*

EXCELLENCE
**3**
*VALUED*

OBJECTIVITY
**5**
*INDEPENDENT*

AUTHENTICITY
**4**
*EXPRESSIVE*

# Primary Fear

Just as the patterns are drawn towards, they also have core fears which they habitually turn away from.

Underneath the behaviors of avoidance rests an underlying fear or concern that the pattern wrestles with.

CONFLICT
**9**
*FRAGMENTATION*

VULNERABILITY
**8**
*CONTROLLED*

ERROR
**1**
*REPROACH*

BOREDOM
**7**
*TRAPPED*

AVOIDS
(What the pattern most turns away from)

SELF-FOCUS
**2**
*REJECTED*

*FEARS*
(The underlying concern)

DANGER
**6**
*ANNIHILATION*

FAILURE
**3**
*WORTHLESS*

INTRUSION
**5**
*INADEQUACY*

INSIGNIFICANCE
**4**
*ABANDONMENT*

# Type Attributes

The combination of core aims and fears results in common or likely attributes. The expression of these may vary depending on the individual's experience, conditioning and personal ways of being.

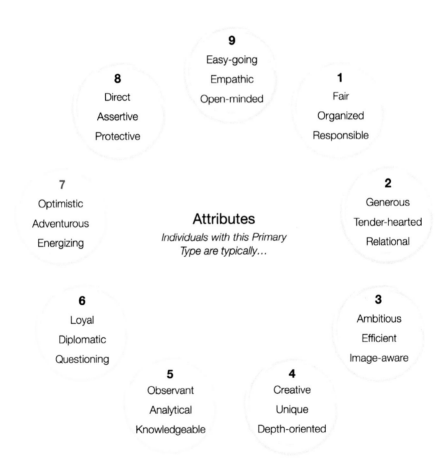

**9**
Easy-going
Empathic
Open-minded

**8**
Direct
Assertive
Protective

**1**
Fair
Organized
Responsible

**7**
Optimistic
Adventurous
Energizing

**Attributes**
*Individuals with this Primary Type are typically...*

**2**
Generous
Tender-hearted
Relational

**6**
Loyal
Diplomatic
Questioning

**3**
Ambitious
Efficient
Image-aware

**5**
Observant
Analytical
Knowledgeable

**4**
Creative
Unique
Depth-oriented

# Type Challenges

The challenges represent common or likely ways in which individuals with this Primary Type get stuck, or get in their own way. Similar to the attributes, the expression of these challenges vary from person to person.

**9**
Merging
Numbing
Indolence

**8**
Controlling
Vengeance
Excess

**1**
Righteousness
Resentment
Critique

**7**
Escapism
Scattered
Rose-colored

**Challenges**
*Individuals with this Primary Type may get stuck in…*

**2**
Hidden agendas
Over-extending
Enabling others

**6**
Skepticism
Catastrophizing
Indecision

**3**
Chasing success
Cutting corners
Spinning the truth

**5**
Withdrawal
Detachment
Narrow-focus

**4**
Melancholy
Dramaticizing
Discontent

# Position

The Position is the Primary Type's default way of addressing conflict. There are three habitual responses of which each pattern will have a primary, secondary and tertiary preference.

All three positions exist in each person
in differing degrees and balances,
a preferred yet variable directionality
moving in accordance with shifting circumstances.
They live alongside the day-to-day relations and negotiations
and amidst the plethora of wants, needs and agendas
that make up a given moment.

| POSITION | TYPES | DIRECTION |
|---|---|---|
| ASSERTIVE | 3 - 7 - 8 | Toward |
| WITHDRAWN | 4 - 5 - 9 | Away |
| RECEPTIVE | 1 - 2 - 6 | With |

Note—on the following page you can see that the three Positions contain a pattern from each of the Centers of Intelligence. In other words, the three types that comprise each 'Position' contain a pattern from the Head, Heart and Gut Triads.

**Assertive** - *Toward*
Taking direct action
to manage or guide
the tension.

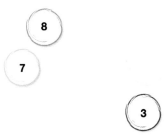

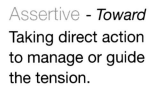

**Withdrawn** - *Away*
Removing or distancing
oneself from the tension
or present moment.

**Receptive** - *With*
Alining with,
or yielding to
the sources of tension.

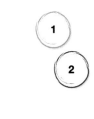

# Approach

The Approach is the Primary Type's way of staying on track with frustrations. The Approach represents how the individual typically directs attention when things aren't going their way. There are three habitual focuses of which each Pattern will have a primary, secondary and tertiary preference.

All three approaches develop in each person
to differing degrees and balances
emerging as an immediate, adaptive way
of reducing, tempering or alchemizing
the distressed situation, which
despite hopes and plans, is now off-kilter
and surely in need of adjustment.

| APPROACH | TYPES | CULTIVATES |
|---|---|---|
| POSITIVITY | 7 - 9 - 2 | Optimism |
| COMPETENCY | 1 - 3 - 5 | Capacity |
| IMMEDIACY | 4 - 6 - 8 | Readiness |

Note—on the following page you can see that the three Approaches contain a pattern from each of the Centers of Intelligence. In other words, the three types that comprise each 'Approach' contain a pattern from the Head, Heart and Gut Triads.

## Positivity - *Optimism*
The desire to see
the bright side;
looking up, finding hope.

## Competency - *Capacity*
Turning towards one's
own capabilities;
emphasizing work or output.

## Immediacy - *Readiness*
The urge to engage;
being inclined to
respond or react.

# Type Template

In the remainder of this section are the details of the Pattern Sets and Instinct Sets for each of the Nine Types.

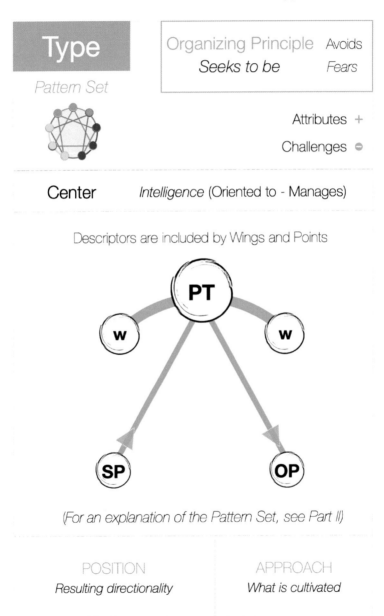

| Type | Organizing Principle | Avoids |
| --- | --- | --- |
| *Pattern Set* | *Seeks to be* | *Fears* |

Attributes +

Challenges ⊖

Center — *Intelligence* (Oriented to - Manages)

Descriptors are included by Wings and Points

**PT**

**W**          **W**

**SP**          **OP**

*(For an explanation of the Pattern Set, see Part II)*

POSITION
*Resulting directionality*

APPROACH
*What is cultivated*

The flow of these pages represents how the energy of the Instincts rests underneath the Pattern Set and is always filtered through the Primary Type.

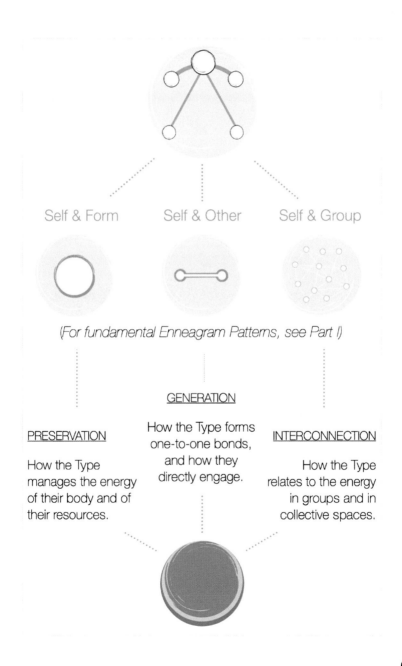

Self & Form          Self & Other          Self & Group

*(For fundamental Enneagram Patterns, see Part I)*

GENERATION

PRESERVATION

How the Type
manages the energy
of their body and of
their resources.

How the Type forms
one-to-one bonds,
and how they
directly engage.

INTERCONNECTION

How the Type
relates to the energy
in groups and in
collective spaces.

INTEGRITY    Error
*Structured*    *Reproach*

Fair, Organized, Responsible  +

Righteousness, Resentment, Critique  ⊖

Gut Type    *Somatic Intelligence* (Fairness - Anger)

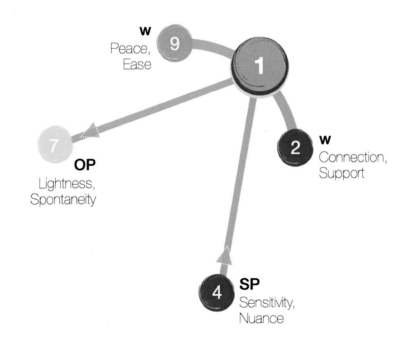

**w**
Peace,
Ease

**OP**
Lightness,
Spontaneity

**w**
Connection,
Support

**SP**
Sensitivity,
Nuance

RECEPTIVE
*Moves "with" order,
complies with what is right*

COMPETENCY
*Capacity for
Improvement*

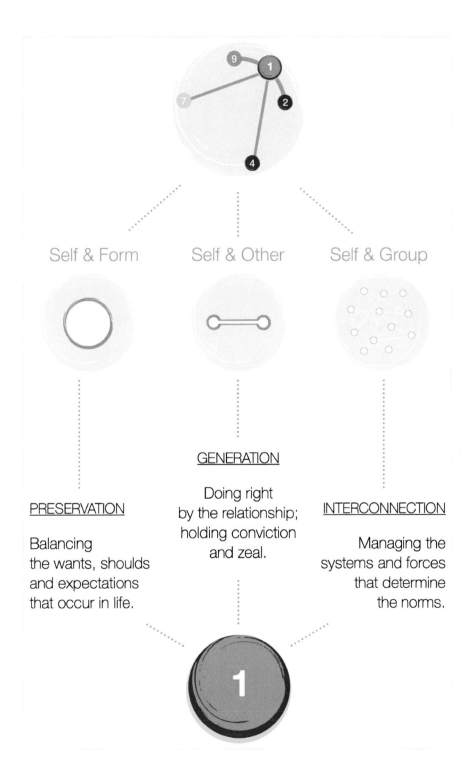

Self & Form

Self & Other

Self & Group

GENERATION

PRESERVATION

Doing right
by the relationship;
holding conviction
and zeal.

Balancing
the wants, shoulds
and expectations
that occur in life.

INTERCONNECTION

Managing the
systems and forces
that determine
the norms.

# Type 2

| CONNECTION | Self-focus |
|:---:|:---:|
| *Helpful* | *Rejected* |

Generous, Tender-hearted, Relational +

Hidden agendas, Over-extending, Enabling others ⊖

## Heart Type *Emotional Intelligence* (Worthiness - Shame)

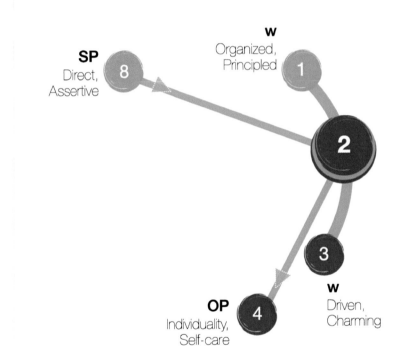

**w**
Organized,
Principled ①

**SP**
Direct,
Assertive ⑧

**2**

**3**

**w**
Driven,
Charming

**OP**
Individuality,
Self-care ④

| RECEPTIVE | POSITIVITY |
|:---:|:---:|
| *Moves "with" others,* | *Optimism for* |
| *adapts self for the relationship* | *people's potential* |

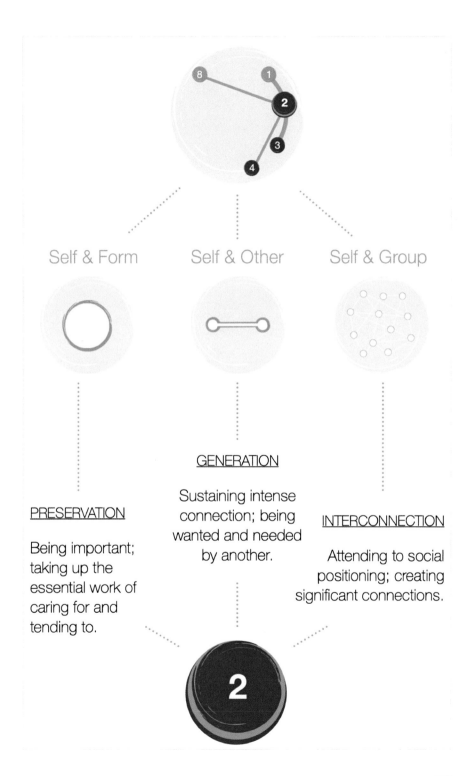

Self & Form

Self & Other

Self & Group

GENERATION

PRESERVATION

Sustaining intense
connection; being
wanted and needed
by another.

INTERCONNECTION

Being important;
taking up the
essential work of
caring for and
tending to.

Attending to social
positioning; creating
significant connections.

## Type 3

| EXCELLENCE | Failure |
|---|---|
| *Valued* | *Worthless* |

Ambitious, Efficient, Image-aware +

Chasing success, Cutting corners, Spinning the truth −

**Heart Type** *Emotional Intelligence* (Worthiness - Shame)

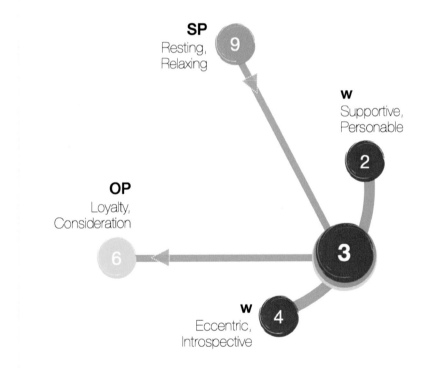

**SP**
Resting,
Relaxing
9

**w**
Supportive,
Personable
2

**OP**
Loyalty,
Consideration
6

3

**w**
Eccentric,
Introspective
4

ASSERTIVE
*Moves "toward" goals,
wants to be seen*

COMPETENCY
*Capacity for work
and productivity*

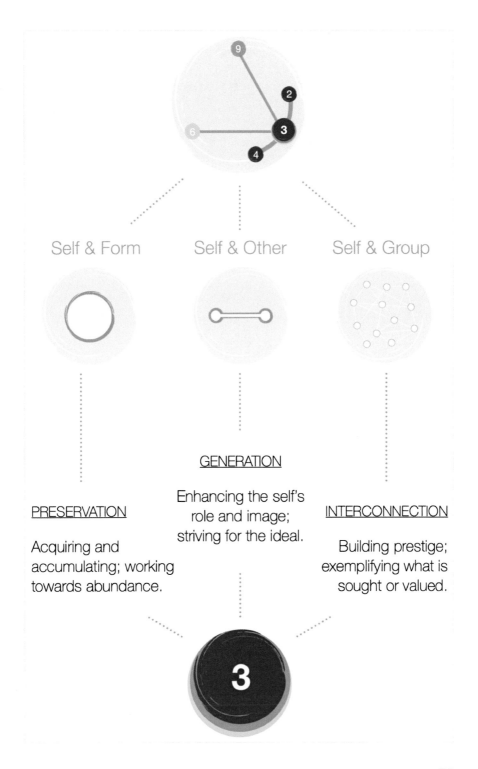

Self & Form

Self & Other

Self & Group

GENERATION

Enhancing the self's
role and image;
striving for the ideal.

PRESERVATION

Acquiring and
accumulating; working
towards abundance.

INTERCONNECTION

Building prestige;
exemplifying what is
sought or valued.

3

## Type 4

*Pattern Set*

Creative, Unique, Depth-oriented  +

Melancholy, Dramaticizing, Discontent  ⊖

**Heart Type**  *Emotional Intelligence* (Worthiness - Shame)

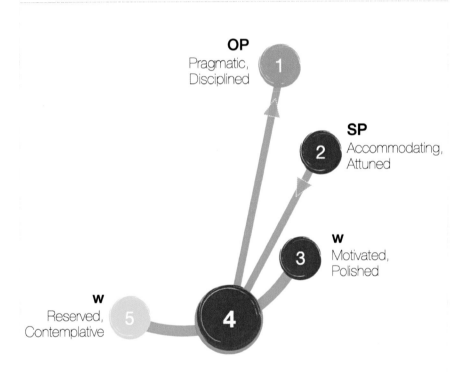

**OP**
Pragmatic,
Disciplined

**SP**
Accommodating,
Attuned

**w**
Motivated,
Polished

**w**
Reserved,
Contemplative

WITHDRAWN
*Moves "away", differentiates,
prefers the inner landscape*

IMMEDIACY
*Readiness for
emotional exchange*

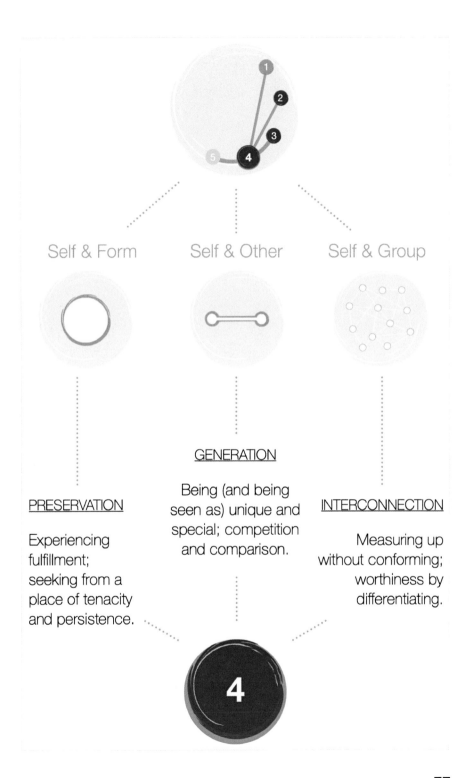

Self & Form

Self & Other

Self & Group

GENERATION

Being (and being seen as) unique and special; competition and comparison.

PRESERVATION

Experiencing fulfillment; seeking from a place of tenacity and persistence.

INTERCONNECTION

Measuring up without conforming; worthiness by differentiating.

4

# Type 5

| OBJECTIVITY | Intrusion |
|---|---|
| *Independent* | *Inadequacy* |

Observant, Analytical, Knowledgeable  +

Withdrawal, Detachment, Narrow-focus  ⊖

**Head Type**  *Mental Intelligence* (Security - Fear)

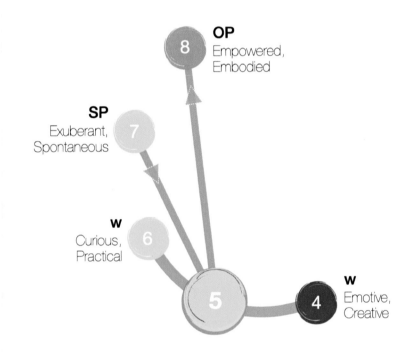

**OP**
Empowered,
Embodied

**SP**
Exuberant,
Spontaneous

**w**
Curious,
Practical

**w**
Emotive,
Creative

WITHDRAWN
*Moves "away" from others,
takes space to process*

COMPETENCY
*Capacity for
investigation*

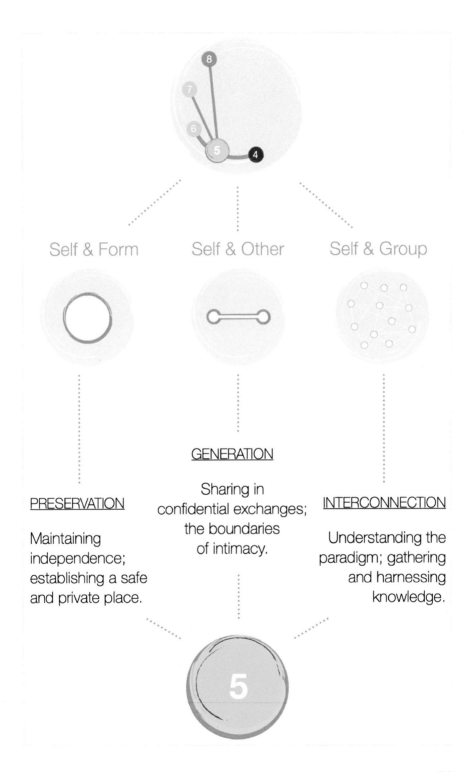

Self & Form

Self & Other

Self & Group

GENERATION

PRESERVATION

Sharing in
confidential exchanges;
the boundaries
of intimacy.

INTERCONNECTION

Maintaining
independence;
establishing a safe
and private place.

Understanding the
paradigm; gathering
and harnessing
knowledge.

# Type 6

| SAFETY | Danger |
|--------|--------|
| *Prepared* | *Annihilation* |

Loyal, Diplomatic, Questioning +

Skepticism, Catastrophizing, Indecision ⊖

Head Type    *Mental Intelligence* (Security - Fear)

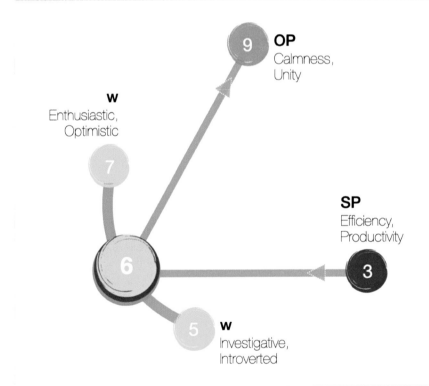

**OP**
Calmness,
Unity

**w**
Enthusiastic,
Optimistic

**SP**
Efficiency,
Productivity

**w**
Investigative,
Introverted

| RECEPTIVE | IMMEDIACY |
|-----------|-----------|
| *Moves "with" the charge, gains protection by aligning* | *Readiness for the counter-position* |

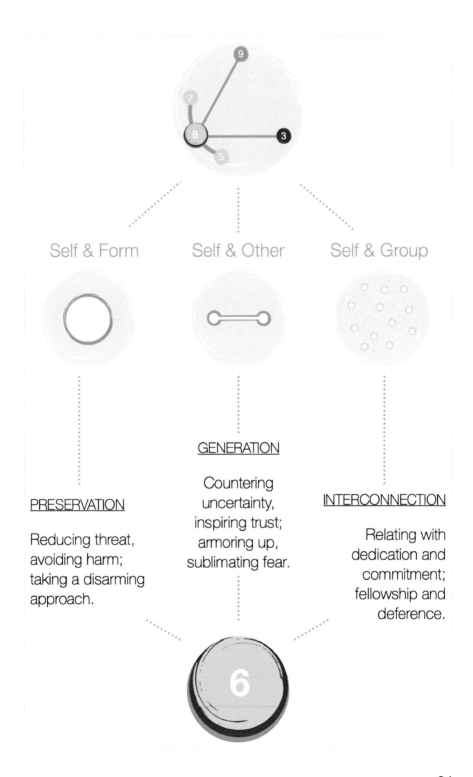

Self & Form

Self & Other

Self & Group

GENERATION

Countering
uncertainty,
inspiring trust;
armoring up,
sublimating fear.

PRESERVATION

Reducing threat,
avoiding harm;
taking a disarming
approach.

INTERCONNECTION

Relating with
dedication and
commitment;
fellowship and
deference.

## Type 7

| ENJOYMENT | Boredom |
|-----------|---------|
| *Excited* | *Trapped* |

Optimistic, Adventurous, Energizing  +

Escapism, Scattered, Rose-colored  ⊖

Head Type    *Mental Intelligence* (Security - Fear)

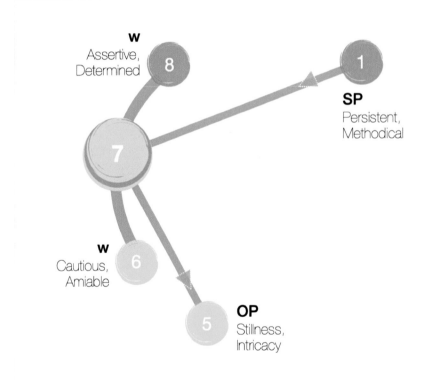

**w**
Assertive, Determined
8

1

**SP**
Persistent, Methodical

7

**w**
Cautious, Amiable
6

5    **OP**
Stillness, Intricacy

| ASSERTIVE | POSITIVITY |
|-----------|------------|
| *Moves "toward" wants, focuses on desires in the present* | *Optimism for fun possibilities* |

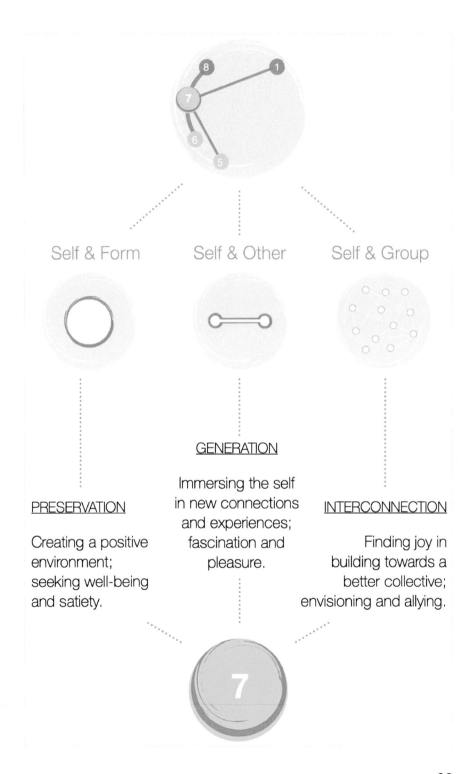

Self & Form

Self & Other

Self & Group

GENERATION

Immersing the self
in new connections
and experiences;
fascination and
pleasure.

PRESERVATION

Creating a positive
environment;
seeking well-being
and satiety.

INTERCONNECTION

Finding joy in
building towards a
better collective;
envisioning and allying.

## Type 8

| STRENGTH | Vulnerability |
|----------|---------------|
| *Powerful* | *Controlled* |

Direct, Assertive, Protective  +

Controlling, Vengeance, Excess  ⊖

Gut Type     *Somatic Intelligence* (Fairness - Anger)

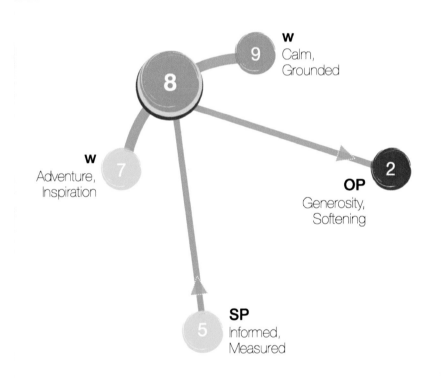

**w**
Calm,
Grounded

**w**
Adventure,
Inspiration

**OP**
Generosity,
Softening

**SP**
Informed,
Measured

| ASSERTIVE | IMMEDIACY |
|-----------|-----------|
| *Moves "toward", takes up space, emphasizes their truth* | *Readiness for confrontation* |

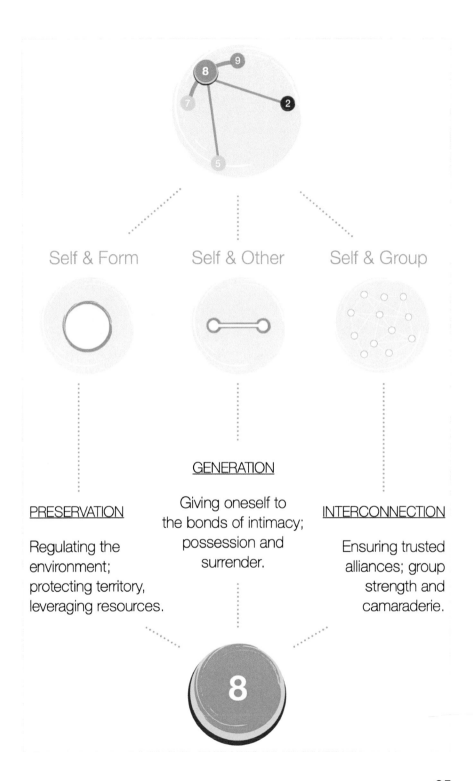

Self & Form

Self & Other

Self & Group

GENERATION

PRESERVATION

Giving oneself to
the bonds of intimacy;
possession and
surrender.

INTERCONNECTION

Regulating the
environment;
protecting territory,
leveraging resources.

Ensuring trusted
alliances; group
strength and
camaraderie.

8

## Type 9

PEACE    Conflict
*Comfortable*    *Fragmentation*

Easy-going, Empathic, Open-minded   +

Merging, Numbing, Indolence   ⊖

Gut Type    *Somatic Intelligence* (Fairness - Anger)

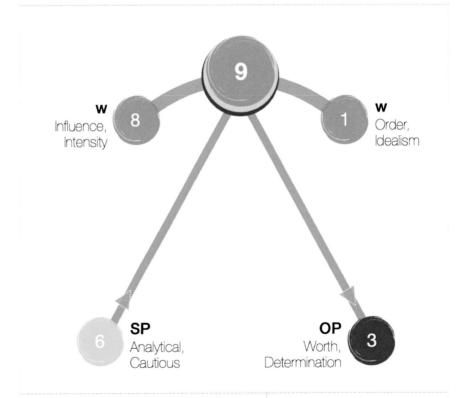

**w**
Influence,
Intensity

**8**

**9**

**1**

**w**
Order,
Idealism

**6**

**SP**
Analytical,
Cautious

**OP**
Worth,
Determination

**3**

WITHDRAWN
*Moves "away" from discord,
seeks a calmer environment*

POSITIVITY
*Optimism for life
and outcomes*

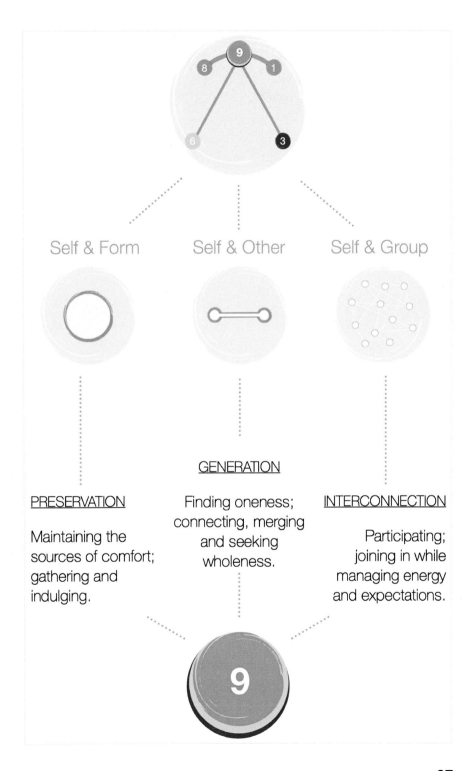

Self & Form

Self & Other

Self & Group

GENERATION

PRESERVATION

Finding oneness;
connecting, merging
and seeking
wholeness.

INTERCONNECTION

Maintaining the
sources of comfort;
gathering and
indulging.

Participating;
joining in while
managing energy
and expectations.

# Triads

## Gut - *Somatic Intelligence*

**Manages: Anger**
Oriented to: Fairness

Senses, Impulses,
Order, Structure

## Heart - *Emotional Intelligence*

**Manages: Shame**
Oriented to: Worthiness

Feelings, Connections,
Perceptions, Aesthetics

## Head - *Mental Intelligence*

**Manages: Fear**
Oriented to: Security

Thinking, Reasoning,
Analyzing, Ideating

*(For more on the Centers of Intelligence, see Part I)*

# Glossary of Terms

The terms here are arranged in the same order as they've been presented in the book. The definitions are written succinctly to serve as a high-level reminder.

<u>Part I - The Patterns</u>
*The Energy and Intelligences that shape personality*

Energy - The force that causes the movement of all things.

Instinct - The application of energy towards surviving and thriving.

    Self & Form - The preservation of energy related to one's body and resources.

    Self & Other - The generation of energy via direct engagement.

    Self & Group - The interconnected energy present in groups and spaces.

Instinct Set - The three instincts in every individual arranged with a primary, secondary and tertiary preference.

*Part I continued*

Centers - The three Centers of Intelligence in every individual that allow for the understanding and processing of information.

Gut - The somatic intelligence found in senses, impulses, order and structure. The gut manages anger and is oriented towards fairness.

Heart - The emotional intelligence found in feelings, connections, perceptions and aesthetics. The heart manages shame and is oriented towards worthiness.

Head - The mental intelligence found in thinking, reasoning, analyzing and ideating. The head manages fear and is oriented towards security.

Triads - The three Primary Types that makeup each of the three Centers of Intelligence.

The Enneagram - A map of the nine interconnected patterns of personality.

## Part II - The Types
*The archetypal patterns of The Enneagram*

Pattern - A repeated, intelligible aspect of personality that supports the overarching strategy and structure around which it is organized.

Type Set - The five patterns that makeup an Enneagram Type. The Primary Type is connected to two Wings and two Lines.

> Primary Type - The personality pattern at the core of the individual. The Primary Type is a strategy organized around seeking and avoidance.

> Wings - The two patterns adjacent to the Primary Type. Individuals will typically lean towards one wing more than the other.

> Lines - The two patterns that each type is connected to via the lines of the Enneagram symbol.

> Support Point - The pattern the Primary Type accesses when needing reinforcement.

> Open Point - The pattern that allows for integration and equilibrium in the Primary Type.

## Part III - The Context
*The impact of life and circumstance on personality*

Awareness - That which can observe without judgement; the essence; the key to understanding and growth.

Habituation - The learned, cyclical patterns that are strengthened through repetition.

Origins - The nature, nurture and existential crossroads that comprise one's beginnings.

Narratives - The stories that are at the heart of what it means to be alive and to be progressing along the journey.

Processing - The work of attending to, integrating and aligning that which is occurring in the Centers of Intelligence.

Holding Space - The presence that opens the grounds for that which needs to arise; the allowing for that which is calling out to be seen, felt and known.

Intentionality - The active and informed process of striving for value-aligned outcomes.

Relationships - The sacred space from which the self is reflected, experienced and known.

Personal - That which can only be known and faced by the individual.

Universal - That which transcends the personal; the wisdom living in the collective.

d

*Key details of the nine Primary Types*

Organizing Principle - The core aspect of personality that the Primary Type is built around.

Seeks - That which motivates the Primary Type; the preferred path forward.

Avoids - What the pattern turns away from; what the type experiences as most threatening.

Fear - The underlying concern; the pain that is at the root of the pattern.

Attributes - Characteristics that are common in individuals of that Primary Type.

Challenges - Where the Primary Type gets in their own way; where individuals with the pattern may get stuck.

Position - The three ways of addressing conflict, of which each individual will contain a primary, secondary and tertiary preference.

Assertive - Taking direct action to manage or guide the tension.

Withdrawn - Removing or distancing oneself from the tension or present moment.

Receptive - Aligning with or yielding to the sources of tension.

Approach - The three ways of staying on track with frustrations, of which each individual will contain a primary, secondary and tertiary preference.

Positivity - The desire to see the bright side; looking up and finding hope.

Competency - Turning towards one's own capabilities; emphasizing work or output.

Immediacy - The urge to engage; being inclined to respond or react.

# Acknowledgments

Thank you to my beloved, Luisa BenAmi.
You are my light and my love,
my anchor to what matters most.

To my feline counterpart Burt—
whom I immediately knew
I was subservient to that fateful moment we met;
'tis his 8-ness that rings supreme.

To our lil chihuahua, Soya.
There are not words of beauty
deep enough nor divine enough
to grace the fur from which her light radiates.

To our most recent addition, Nina…
tortitude waves of innocence
splashing upon the sweet-playful-purity
only to topple over and tuck back in upon
that steady and comforting shore.

Thank you to the International Enneagram Association for being a place of deep learning and connection, and for their work and excellence in building the Enneagram community.

To the EnneaApp users, subscribers and collaborators who have helped me find my voice. I am filled with deep gratitude for all the teaching, sharing and connection over the years.

Special thank you to the proof readers, who lended such sincere support and friendship amidst the process. Thank you Luisa BenAmi, Jack Ringel, Veronica Dieda, Christina Dickinson, Katie Mason and Lori Ohlson.

Made in the USA
Middletown, DE
25 January 2023

23162477R00062